I0152347

ALISONOWARD

Allegheny River Trip Journal

June 1937

Howard Zahniser

Table of Contents

A Conservation Giant Who Emerged From our Midst

Fifteen years ago I was researching and writing a paper about wilderness designation in the Allegheny National Forest for the Natural Areas Journal when renowned wilderness historian Doug Scott reviewed a draft of my manuscript, and we began emailing. Doug had a hunch that Wilderness Act of 1964 author Howard Zahniser, who I mentioned in my paper, was from this part of Pennsylvania, and checked with Zahniser's son Ed in West Virginia. Ed confirmed that his father indeed hailed from the small Forest County town of Tionesta!

When I learned this news, I was immediately struck by the enormity of the connection. The primary author of the Wilderness Act was from our own Allegheny National Forest, but few people locally seemed to be aware of it then. The man whose vision has seen nearly 110 million acres of wilderness on federal public lands permanently protected—including the 368-acre Allegheny Islands and 8,630-acre Hickory Creek Wilderness in Pennsylvania — was a local.

Howard Zahniser spent his formative youth and teen years in Tionesta, in a setting that offered numerous opportunities for a young man to explore nature and observe many species of wildlife across the verdant landscape. The family lived on the steep pitch of Bridge Street, above the main street, three blocks from the Allegheny River. (The present bridge is now located upstream of Bridge Street.) Zahniser worked his first job at The Forest Press newspaper in town. He and his wife Alice are laid to rest along the banks of his beloved Allegheny River, near other family members, in Tionesta's Riverside Cemetery. His natural headstone, collected from the surrounding forest, is the only one in the cemetery that grows lichens.

Zahniser, or "Zahnie" as many knew him, executive director of The Wilderness Society from 1945 until his passing in 1964, was a Washington, D.C.-based conservationist; an inside-the-Beltway activist and lobbyist. From TWS headquarters in the nation's capital he oversaw the organization's affairs, lobbied against numerous threats to wilderness, and for years campaigned fervently for the wilderness bill that he drafted in 1956. Though his affinity for the Adirondack Mountains is perhaps better known to some, throughout his life Zahniser frequently returned to Tionesta with his family where he found escape and serenity in the surrounding Penn's Woods.

In June of 1937 Zahnie and his wife Alice took a 14-day, 100-mile trip down the

Allegheny River from Olean, New York to Tionesta in their canoe, the Alisonoward (a clever amalgamation of their first names), which could then be done continuously as this was before the days of the Kinzua Dam above Warren. He kept a journal of their experiences during this journey, also titled Alisonoward, which you now hold in your hands. It provokes the imagination to think that as the Zahnisers canoed past Baker, Crull's, No Name and other islands that June, and in fact camped one night on Thompson's Island, that these islands would some fifty years after their trip be included in America's National Wilderness Preservation System as part of the Allegheny Islands Wilderness — as a result of Zahniser's subsequent work.

The Wilderness Act, widely considered to be the most artfully-worded legislation in U.S. statute, provides mechanisms for setting aside significant tracts of federal land in perpetuity for primitive recreation, hunting, and fishing opportunities. No resource extraction or permanent developments are allowed. Wilderness, according to the Act, is a place "…where the earth and its community of life are untrammeled by man, where man himself is a visitor who does not remain."

Through more than 100 bipartisan acts of Congress over the last 50 years, the amount of wilderness designated nationwide has grown from 9 million acres to nearly 110 million acres. There are now 758 wilderness areas in 44 states and Puerto Rico — with more to come. Wilderness areas are important because they are the only lands in the country where nature is by law the primary influence across the landscape, and where threatened and endangered species can find undisturbed refuge and high-quality habitat. They are expanses where humans have had the humility to acknowledge that we do not have all the answers, and that natural processes will always better steward our wildlands in the absence of human intervention — nature is never 'doing it wrong,' no matter what.

Zahnie died in his sleep at his home in Hyattsville, Maryland on May 5, 1964 just six days after testifying at the final hearing on his wilderness bill, and a few months before it was signed into law by President Lyndon Johnson in the White House Rose Garden on September 3 at a ceremony attended by Zahnie's widow Alice in his stead. The bill had gone through dozens of revisions and 18 public hearings, and Zahniser was an active participant throughout the process, personally guiding the landmark legislation through the labyrinth of Congress. Filled with the conviction that the cause for the wilderness bill was just, he was a tireless advocate to the end. "Confident of his own views, he was unfailingly polite in his dealings with others, even those who strongly disagreed with him. For him, making room for wild lands was a matter of inclusion, of enlarging an old and deep-seated outlook that saw the utility of natural resources as paramount," wrote biographer Mark Harvey in his 2005 biography, Wilderness Forever: Howard Zahniser and the Path to the Wilderness Act. The wilderness bill had passed the Senate 73 to 12 at the time of Zahniser's death, and it later passed the House by the overwhelming margin of 373 to 1.

All the while he labored over the wilderness bill, Zahnie was troubled by the consequences of the construction of the aforementioned Kinzua Dam here in Pennsylvania, particularly as it concerned the Seneca Nation of Indians. He once told his son Ed he regretted that his push for the passage of the Wilderness Act prevented his being able to do more to contest the dam and flooding of Seneca lands. Zahnie had a particular aversion to inappropriately located dams. In the early 1950s, in his capacity with The Wilderness Society, he and others successfully challenged an ill-conceived plan to construct a dam at the confluence of the Green and Yampa Rivers in Colorado's breathtaking Dinosaur National Monument. The momentum generated by the campaign's success was immediately employed by Zahnie and others to launch into the campaign for the wilderness bill.

Years ago, Ed Zahniser gave me some 1949 U.S. Geological Survey topographic maps of Pennsylvania. They were given to his father by then-Wilderness Society President Benton MacKaye. MacKaye, who originated the Appalachian Trail concept in 1921, used these maps to plot what is now the North Country National Scenic Trail through Pennsylvania. Today's North Country Trail traverses the Allegheny National Forest for 95 miles, including through several areas proposed for wilderness designation by Friends of Allegheny Wilderness.

MacKaye's USGS Kinzua Quadrangle includes today's proposed Tracy Ridge Wilderness, before Kinzua Dam created the Allegheny Reservoir. The map shows a sprawling landscape, largely roadless in character, with the river untrammeled by a dam. Now professionally matted and framed, the map, one of my most trea-sured possessions, hangs prominently on my living room wall. Because of the land-scape it depicts — and its chain of owner-ship — this map is constant inspiration for my own wilderness advocacy work.

My family has a long history in the Al-legheny region. On my paternal grandfather's side, my ancestors arrived in Warren County from Sweden in the late 1800s to work in the leather tanneries. My paternal grandmother Evelyn Winifred Gannoe Johnson's family arrived in McKean County during the 1700s. They were all of course familiar with the pre-Kinzua Dam Allegheny River. In 2003 my grandmother published a Gannoe family history in which she wrote the following of her experience on the river as a child in the 1920s:

"Aunt Flossie and Uncle Merle lived at Hemlock, Pennsylvania, along the Allegheny River near Warren. What fun our cousins, my sisters and I had playing in the water on 'inner tubes,' rowing the boat and hiking in the woods.... There was plenty of room for picnics, family reunions, etc. There was always a rowboat available for us to use. We kids spent many happy hours rowing up and down the Allegheny River. It was especially beautiful in the fall with the hills rising high on either side glowing with brilliant colors."

The construction of the dam flooded one third of the Seneca's reservation lands, breaching the 1794 Treaty of Canandaigua, New York, which had been signed by President George Washington and Chief Cornplanter of the Senecas. Further, the Cornplanter tract was a 1,500-acre perpetual land grant given to Chief Cornplanter and his descendants just inside Pennsylvania along the west shore of the Allegheny River. Much of this tract, too, including an ancestral cemetery and final resting place for Chief Cornplanter, was lost to the Allegheny Reservoir. The Senecas were compensated for the loss of their lands through the establishment of Jimersontown next to the city of Salamanca, New York, and other resettlement areas. As you read through Alisonoward you will find descriptions of now submerged Seneca lands, as well as those of towns like Corydon and Kinzua where homes were lost to many other people as well.

When Ed gave me a copy of his father's journal back in 2000, it was touching to read and think about the history of this area, the immensely complicated network of competing interests in the Allegheny National Forest region, and the gravity of the magnanimous work that Howard Zahniser went on to do later in life. Though there will always be timbering and other uses present here, as there should be, it seems disrespectful that merely less than two percent of the 513,000-acre national forest near Zahnie's home has achieved the status of protected wilderness under the legislation he labored for so long and so hard. There are so many special areas here that could and should be permanently protected. For example, today, on lands around the Allegheny Reservoir that the Zahnisers canoed past on a bright June day nearly 80 years ago, we have the opportunity to designate untrammeled roadless tracts such as the 3,022-acre proposed Cornplanter Wilderness and as the 9,705-acre proposed Tracy Ridge Wilderness.

I am grateful that the Zahniser family has agreed to make this journal available to the public in this 50th anniversary year of the Wilderness Act so that others might enjoy reliving this unique pre-Kinzua Dam snapshot in time, written by one of the foremost conservationists in our nation's history. What a joy that we can claim Howard Zahniser as one of our own here on the Allegheny River, and live vicariously through his keen observations recorded long ago.

Special thanks to Tara Bauschard Munch for her attention to detail in transcribing Alisonoward into electronic format; and to Ed Zahniser for editing the text in preparation for publication, and for suggesting appropriate supplemental content.

— Kirk Johnson,
Friends of Allegheny Wilderness,
Warren, Pennsylvania,
August, 2014

<u>June 20</u> Cloudy in a. m., looked like storm. I got up at 7.45 and made coffee for Heine on eteno stove. My campfire burned all night OK. I took three photos of camp in rather poor light and set up camera in cottage to photograph Phoebes if I get chance. Now 10.15. River has receded considerably, is back beyond a stick I put in day before yesterday. Cuckoo is cu-cu-cu-ing. Phoebe is chirping. Flies are buzzing around me. This is reading. Sun is coming out. — I discovered nest of cuckoo in bushes back of two maples.

June 12

As I was parking car Sam Wilson, 3100
Conn. Ave., Apt. 245 came along with a
female red-tailed hawk captured around
1st of May. I took two photos.

About noon we left, mileage 20314, with
about 10 mi. already driven after a full
tank. . . . I had been to town for duffel
bag, knapsack, & canteen. From Frederick went n. and to Greencastle by way of
Blue Ridge Summit & Penn-Mar, our first
time that way. Top is down.

Mercersburg, about _____ , got 7 1/2
gals. Amoco and ate lunch. Mileage
20419.

Philipsburg, near 6, mileage 20515, got 7
gals. Am. 1 qt. oil. Mr. Robertson knew
Uncle Jake's family.

At [Smethport] got 1 qt. oil and bundled
up more. At St. Marys we left AAA route
& went via Emporium. Made good time.
In [Smethport] at 8 or little after, and
Via Larrabee and Portville reached Cuba
Lake at about 9.15, mileage 20653. Had a
pleasant evening with Letha, Raymond &
Erla May. Letha had some chili con carne
waiting for us & it warmed us.

June 13

Up fairly early. Fooled around with duffel bags. Erla May and I drove around to [Davis], to talk about canoe. On way around lake saw 2 small ducks, maybe teal. Davis sent canoe over, and saw it as it was being paddled across the lake. I tried it out & then Raymond & I were in it, & Alice and I. We put the load in once. O.K. Rices went home late in p.m. Rain began. Alice & I had a cozy time. Soon after dinner (late) we went to bed.

June 14

We had a good time celebrating Alice's birthday. There was rain most of day. I went out in canoe alone in rain, and then we both went for a long paddle (saw a merganser [?] and 2 teal [?]) and swam when we came back. In p.m. we went to Cuba for groceries and bought a lamp & drainer as a present to leave in the cottage. The sunset was beautiful, the water quiet for the first time in the day. I sat up reading. Yesterday and today I have read most of three books on Allegheny State Park—geology, geography, ecology of birds—and some in Palgrave and the Bible.

June 15

We paddled about a bit and swam and I
took canoe over to Davis for delivery to
Olean. We prepared to leave Cuba Lake.
On our way to Letha's we stopped at Oil
Spring of the Senecas and took 2 photos.
In Olean we arranged at filling station
for reception of canoe. Arrived at Rices
before they did. Raymond sharpened our
axe and knife. We had good dinner &
some archery and baseball till dark. Then
some music and Raymond showed us his
movies—fine pictures of oil-well opera-
tions & trips they had taken. One good
shot of my grandfather. Erla May enter-
tained us with her cat Snooks.

June 16

After big breakfast we packed into Rice's
car & Letha, Erla May & a neighbor boy
took us to Olean. We bought groceries in
Bradford—$5.27 & $1.38 and a sterno
outfit, 5¢ and 25¢. Letha and Erla May
left us in Olean with good wishes. We had
($1.15) dinner & bought apples, carrots,
etc., 54¢ & Noxema & tooth paste, 69¢.

From filling station near bridge we packed
our things and loaded above bridge with
2 men and some boys on hand to watch.
One man thought our canoe pretty frag-
ile. Man at filling station told me about
channels. Alice took my picture in canoe
after loaded.

At 2 p.m. we pushed off. A kingfisher followed us down the river about 4 miles. We saw many green herons. One so close in swampy area about across from Vandalia, that we stopped and stretched our legs. This is marked 2 on our map. There were many yellow flags in one bunch and 1 large blue flag. We went on with some excitement in rapids and around islands. Alice spied a woodchuck along bank. We went up the Tunungwant Creek about 1 1/2 mile & camped on west bank. Creek much deeper than I supposed & the mosquitoes were so bad that we camped hastily in a good place [marked 3 on our maps] except for lack of spring water. Stopped at 6.30. Put up tent & Alice had ham, chicken noodle soup, & fruit cocktail & carrots (raw). Citronella stopped the mosquitoes. To bed about 9. Locomotive kept us awake! An owl or flying squirrel made a noise like a raspy rattle—something like a kingfisher's rattle with a buzz in it. Rain began about 3 and lasted till 7.

[**Marginal note to June 16**: Boys threw stones with slings.]

June 17

I got up in rain & built fire & made Alice coffee & we ate an orange. Rain eased up & breeze helped us dry things. Had pancakes & bacon & coffee about 1.30. Saw a large black beetle eating a green "measuring worm." Maybe the "squirrel or owl" last night was a green heron. We started down the Tunungwant & as we did rain started again. We had a thrill going through pilings under railroad trestle in swift current, just above mouth of stream. As we reached the Allegheny rain began to pour down. River was high & no good places to land, but when downpour grew worse we pulled up under a large overhanging beech tree and held on to the roots. We sat there quite a while & then pushed on. We stopped some ways farther down & looked for a camping place, but the place was low & no water for drinking in evidence. Saw deer tracks there. So after a change to dry clothes we paddled on. Fish frequently jumping from water interested us, and sandpipers were numerous along the bank or skimming over the river. We stopped along the shale bank of a railroad on west shore and ate a can of beans and some fruit. (5 on map) I walked a ways for a canteen of water. Saw a butterfly along railroad whirling in cinders. It was not hurt. I wonder if it was making nest. On way back I picked some strawberries. We paddled on, looking for a camping place. I could not use map because of rain. Just beyond (5) what seemed like mouth of stream from distance turned out to be a channel of the river around an island. We went in, but the place was not suitable, and the river on ahead that way seemed dangerous.

So we paddled back up to other channel and in doing it had a hard thrilling pull. During it I got 2 sights of a great blue heron, but had no chance even to mention it then. Soon we saw an old abandoned house as we were rounding a bend to the left. The house was on the right bank, and we managed to stop there & land. The house had burned about 5 weeks ago & boy & man happened to be there looking place over. We learned it was Great Valley. I walked up with them and bought milk, eggs, pail, dishpan, pepsa-cola, Hershey bars, aspirin. Right across the river we found a good camping place, (6) on map. Indian land, of course, but Boy Scouts of Salamanca (2mi. down river) had built a cottage there. Abandoned some time ago. Two fishermen there when we arrived. I set up tent, and built fire, and Alice made hash and we were glad to eat. Our bed-clothes were dry all right. We had cocoa late and went to bed about 12 in tent. Mosquitoes bad. Still raining. Rained all night, but we kept warm & dry, though some clothes got wet.

June 18

Spent whole day at "Riverside Camp," drying out bedclothes & tent. Black-billed cuckoo, first thing I heard in a.m. Phoebes have nest in porch of cottage & they are of course disturbed, afraid of our things when we go away. River is very high,

Alice Zahniser cooking over an open fire at Lake Solitude, Cloud Peak Primitive Area, Bighorn Mountains, Wyoming, 1956. Alice was the expert logistician behind her family's many wilderness experiences that buttressed Howard's wilderness preservation work. She was "the Mother Teresa of outdoor cooking over open wood fires."
Photo courtesy of Ed Zahniser.

even somewhat bowed. Has risen 3 or 4 feet or more since last night. (Now 5.30). Driftwood & debris interesting. I arose early & made coffee for Alice and fixed oranges. Ate berries myself too. Then Alice got "breakfast" with eggs and dried beef gravy. We didn't get up till 10.30 and ate breakfast at some after noon. We have our fire on concrete porch under roof. We ate about 7, ham, fried potatoes, tomato soup, tea, bread & butter. I made up the bed while Alice washed dishes. It was still raining & the tent was still wet in some places on floor, partly from leaking I guess but mostly from water collecting in low places under the tent floor. I put ponchos down over floor, then mattresses with ponchos folding up over the bottom. With our car blanket we had enough dry bed clothes but had to get along with only one sheet. Afterwards we sat around the fire & talked, and I cracked some nuts. Alice went to bed about 9.30 and as soon as I had taken care of the fire I did too. I took 2 aspirins for day-long headache. Shaved about noon. I got into bed at just 10, and we were thrilled just then to see a long passenger train on the Erie across the river go by — a lighted belt as Blanche Smith said in some of her verse. We had seen it the night before and also then the moon through the clouds, which excit-ed us much, but this night there was no moon, rain.

June 19

I slept well but for a cold back. Was disappointed at 6.30 to see clouds and feel
a cold breeze. So lay til 8 and then got
up and made coffee for Alice & then ate
an orange, drank coffee, and had bread
with butter & brown sugar. Two boys
from Salamanca who were here when
we came returned on a fishing trip about
8.30 but went back as the river was too
high. We were delighted to see the sky
clear up about 9 and a hot sun come
out, though there was a cooling breeze.
One of the most beautiful days I have
ever seen. We soon had everything on
lines or spread out on the ground. Took
the tent down and spread it out in sun
in dry place. Built the fire on riverbank
under large maples and Alice made
cakes and cocoa and cooked bacon and
egg. My back is getting stiff from cutting
so much wood with a small axe.

We had a good meal just at noon and
lots of Karo syrup, and then Alice went
for some drinking water — an explorato-
ry trip through woods and along railroad
tracks to place described by the boys this
a.m. She is not back yet. We have moved
the things away from the phoebes' cor-
ner of the porch, and they seem better
off and happier today, too. I climbed to
roof of Riverside Camp to guide her
back. About 4 o'clock, after building up

fire to boil ham, I took pail & knapsack
and started for water & Salamanca. Got
to Salamanca about 5.15. Bought Sterno, 50¢; flashlight & extra batteries, 54¢;
steak, 60¢; bacon 30¢; groceries — milk,
bread, evaporated milk, 6 eggs, 6 oranges,
can spaghetti, paper napkins, tissue paper,
can peas — 96¢; Fri. Christian Science
Monitor & Sat. [NY] Herald-Tribune,
10¢. Chanced to see Rev. Schroder on
street. Started back about 6.30.

When I got to pail I carried it back a ways
to mt. stream, beautiful. When I got to
place where I marked to leave railroad
and start bushwhacking to camp, I sat
down to rest. Looking up track I thought I
saw Alice standing 1/4 mile away waiting
for me. I discovered I had lost my field
glasses, found them where I had left pail.
What I had seen up the track was a deer,
facing me like a statue, its ears spread
out. I walked on up the track, stopping
now & then to look through glasses. The
deer did not move. When I got within 3
telegraph poles, I left the track, thinking
that I would bring Alice to see it. I called
to her and she came to meet me, bring-
ing camera. We bushwhacked toward
the deer and, coming through a poplar
thicket a pole and a half away from the
deer, saw it still standing like a mounted
specimen. A yellow-throat came right out
in front of us.

It was so late in the evening that I was going to circle around, see if I could get closer while Alice watched through glasses where she was. But the deer seemed disturbed, and I tried to raise camera above bushes and wondering about light. Then the deer turned flank to us, showed white tail. If I had been closer I would have had a good photo even in evening light. But I didn't try. The deer bounded away and as it did made the noise that we both recognized was what we had heard in the night along the Tunungwant.

We returned to camp, built up fire and had ham, boiled potatoes, beets, prunes, tea. I moved the tent under the two maples and we went to bed right after the 10 o'clock flyer passed. There was a bright half moon that threw maple leaf shadows on the tent. Most of the flowers we see are hawkweed, daisies, and buttercups. The river is receding.

June 20

Cloudy in a.m., looked like storms. I got up at 7.45 and made coffee for Alice on sterno stove. My campfire burned all night ok. I took three photos of camp in rather poor light and set up camera in cottage to photograph phoebes if I get chance. Now 10.15. River has receded considerably, is back beyond a stick I put in day before yesterday. Cuckoo is cu-cu-cuing. Phoe-

Campsite of Alice and Howard Zahniser along the Allegheny River near Salamanca, New York, June 1937. Upon close inspection, "Alisonoward" can be seen painted on the bow of their canoe just below the gunwale.

Photo by and courtesy of Alice Zahniser.

be is chirping. Flies are buzzing round
me. Alice is reading. Sun is coming out.
— I discovered nest of cuckoo in bushes
back of two maples. Thinking there was
a nest there I crouched on the ground
and squeaked so Alice could see the bird.
There was no evidence of the bird, but by
chance I found that I was right under the
nest. The bird stayed on while we were
very close and left silently. I then cut an
opening into the bush so we could see it
& photograph it. Then I started to work
on photographing phoebe's nest — a long
undertaking. There was no light on the
nest, which was under the roof. I used
Alice's hand mirror to throw sunlight on
it, and I made a sort of blind behind the
window of the cottage. Then I waited
and frequently had to go out and adjust
mirror.

We had some cornflakes and prunes.
Then took some photos of the cuckoo
on nest, finally getting within 3 feet, but
I doubt that the pictures were good. We
made up a pack and started on a hike
about 2 p.m. Went south to railroad
tracks, then west to stream that is unnamed on my map — butterfly brook
I might suggest, for just inside its valley
we saw seven swallowtails and later 8.
(7 on map) They finally all collected in
one small area and I tried to photograph
them, with a wood sorrel flower too. The
swallowtails had their probosces in the

ground and were exuding a clear colorless
fluid from the other end. One, behaving a
little differently from the rest, was closer to
the ground & quivering its wings.

We followed the stream up as far as it
went and then through old paths and
sometimes bushwhacking came to an old
road and followed it up till it started down
over shoulder. There we left our packs
and went on up the shoulder to [look at]
a sunset, (8 on the map), and climbed an
oak and a sassafras to get good lookouts.
Good view down the wide alley of the
Allegheny & also of the forested plateau
country here. We returned to our packs
and I made a fire & Alice fixed food &
we had broiled steak, fried potatoes,
spaghetti covered with tomatoes, bread,
carrots, Hershey bar & water. We hurried
on down the road. A hermit thrush was
singing. Hill is unnamed but might be
Beefsteak Knob.

We returned through E. edge of Salamanca & railroad tracks, got water in pail
left at brook. While bushwhacking from
railroad to camp we saw deer again, probably same one we saw last night. When
we noticed it, it was bounding away & we
could hear the thumps. We got back to
camp about 8.00 and were soon in bed.
Had a lovely time watching campfire and
coals, hearing river, and trees, and watching lightning, and hearing thunder and

finally rain. Till the 10 o'clock flyer came and we went to sleep.

June 21

We got up to cloudy skies again, disappointed this time. I sat up early in bed trying to take care of butterfly book that had been soaked. After our coffee I built fire on porch and then moved it in front of tent later. A rainy day & I tried to arrange things in tent while Alice was arranging our foodstuff in packs. A terribly strong storm came up about 3 o'clock & it was good thing I was inside. Then the sun came out clear and beautiful. [Marginal note: The river went down about to where it was when we landed.] We paddled across the river and spent about $3 for groceries and 4 pairs of heavy socks. Before going we had hung bedclothes on line and as soon as we had come back & eaten (ham, peas, beets, bacon & ham soup, tea, olives, coke) a storm started up the valley, soon obliterating a very beautiful moon and making weird sunset effects up Great Valley & down the Allegheny Valley. We hurried to get bedclothes in & I held them before the fire till rain began. Only the foot ends were damp. Then we got in ready for the storm. I read aloud "Saturday" in Thoreau's Week. The storm passed over & we got only a little rain. The 10 o'clock train went by at 9.30, we having corrected the watch.

June 22

We saw the sunrise for the first time about
6, but got up to cloudy skies and strong
breeze. Nevertheless we resolved to go on.
Had bacon & eggs after coffee & oranges
and then packed up. During breakfast two
canoers stopped — Biscoe & Singleton
from Pittsburgh. But they soon hurried on
after looking at maps. They had camped
too near river last night & had to move.
River came up again, higher than we have
seen it yet. But about 10 we pushed off
and went rapidly down rough high river
thru Salamanca with no place to stop, and
at mouth of Little Valley Creek, (9) on
map, where water comes through culverts
under railroad track had our first close call
as cross currents, perhaps over an island
in low water made billows higher than
canoe. Train came along just then too.
But, both paddling hard, we kept canoe
headed down stream and all went well.

River is very high, gurgling, satisfied with
its strength. At lower end of horseshoe
bend, (10) on map, we landed on north
bank on edge of cornfield. I took photo
of Alice down stream and also one of
snake on bank. Would have taken more
but it glided into river. Saw large heron.
Kingfishers active here, seem worried at
river. Barn swallows flying about & bank
swallows too I think. Sky is beautifully
blue with large white or bluish cumulus

clouds casting shadows on the hills. We set
up tent temporarily & spread out things
and a strong wind & bright sun are drying
them rapidly. We ate, milk, baked beans,
carrots, bread & butter & brown sugar
(for me) & cake for Alice. There is much
driftwood in river. I watched one bunch
of stuff that looked like an island or a raft.
It went right over fallen tree in channel
& lodged on bank at bend. I spent an
hour or two with sparrows in the field. I
couldn't find the nest but got some good
poses, though my focusing was hasty.

We were somewhat disconcerted by the
river conditions. Alice seemed to want
to go on, but I was afraid of the river.
She was afraid the tent would blow into
the river. So I carried the tent 1/8 mile
across corn patch and set it up near some
trees. Then I succeeded in building a fire
out of some fence posts that were pretty wet to start with, and Alice cooked a
good dinner—tomatoes, spaghetti, ham
& cocoa—the wind quieted down and a
full moon rose across the turbulent river,
over the hill, and spread rough moonlight
on the river. I drove a fence post into the
ground, tied canoe to it, put firewood &
duffel in it, covered it, and we walked over
to our tent and had a lovely time after a
trying day. Moonlight shone in the tent
until a heavy mist came up and blanketed
us. There were many birds about during
the day. The kingfishers seemed much

bothered. I suspect they had a nest in the flooded bank on which we landed. So also, I think with the bank swallows.

June 23

I awoke early but the mist was still heavy and while the good sun was chasing away the mist I read Emerson's essay on Prudence, appreciating highly all of it, but I remember best tonight his statement: If you go to the woods you must feed mosquitoes. I walked out to the camp and was delighted to see that river level had fallen at least 2 feet and the monster had quieted down. I made a fire & coffee, and Alice came, and we had our coffee & oranges. Then while she cooked griddle cakes and bacon I took down the tent.

The sun was very hot. I cut a step in the bank and drove the stake in deep. Then I tied our rope to it, and Alice held the other. So we loaded and about noon shoved off—almost exactly a day after we sought refuge there. Under other conditions it would have been a very enjoyable day, and indeed there are many memorable things about it. There were kingfishers, swallows, green herons, crows, redwings, and yesterday we saw an eagle fly across the sky. The river was in much better travel conditions (for us), but just around the bend we went through some high, billowing & rapid riffles—almost as bad as those yesterday, but these we saw ahead and found them rather thrilling, though frightening. They are at (11) on the map. The river was rough in most places and covered a good many small islands where could see the tops of willow bushes trying to straighten themselves up to the sun. But in a couple of places there were long smooth stretches, and Alice managed the canoe alone for the most part through these. The current was swift. We passed the mouth of Red House Brook and might have turned upstream into it but didn't make up our minds in time.

The river was too high and swift as we went under Quaker Bridge to stop either above or below, and at the mouth of Quaker Run we had our hands full managing the canoe. It was inadvisable to try and stop there. Along the way we saw many birds—a few sandpipers; a catbird singing beautifully on conspicuous dead branch of a bush; a Baltimore oriole in the tip-top of a tree, bright black and gold with a foreground of bright green and a background of beautifully blue sky; and a great blue heron at close range that flew out from along the left bank and on up the stream behind us. Alice watched the heron, but I was having to paddle and watch the river pretty closely and got only two or three good picture glances. The water was deep and rough along the railroad embankment about mouth of Wolf's Run.

After rounding bend at mouth of Pierce Run I expected a stretch of smooth water, and Alice started to do most of the paddling. But the water became very rough and wavy, and both of us had to paddle around the bend.

Then, at (12) on the map, we came into as high and billowy riffles as any we have had. I am sure that from trough to crest they were at least 3 feet high, but they were broad too and the canoe went over them as gracefully as a canoe can. I handled it alone and did only a little paddling, using the paddle mainly as a rudder to keep heading into the riffles. We really enjoyed them. An Indian later said that there is a sort of falls there, and that is certainly what it seemed like. Soon afterwards we approached the bridge at Onoville. We were much burned, baked and dried out in the hot sun and decided to land if possible. It was about 3 p.m. The river was rapid and rather riffly, but I skirted what appeared on the map as an island, keeping on the river side of it and expecting to ease into the triangle of quiet water I have noticed at the down stream end of islands, between the two currents. But, to our delight the area was no longer an island, having filled in on the bank side. We found an absolutely quiet bay with even a little up current at the lower end. The water was high, but we managed to land easily between two trees. This was at (13) on the map.

We left the canoe and walked across the bridge. Sun very hot. We went to a store. While Alice was buying things — $2.38, I believe, I talked with little girl. Said her father owns store, her mother the tavern. Then I talked with group of Indians working on bridge approach, about the river, game, and Mary Jemison & Indians. One old fellow had a great deal of lore. I looked for a camping place & found it in field back of church and toward river. [**Marginal note:** Saw cowbird at entrance to field.]

Put up the tent after getting Alice and we carried canoe & duffle to campsite. We washed and put on street clothes and went to tavern for supper—60¢. On way we talked to boy from house near us. Long walk to tavern. We returned to store, wrote cards, got our groceries, and came to camp. Alice made up the bed, blowing up mattresses, too, while I wrote in the journal. Just as we were going to bed we saw the aura of a full moon coming over Round Top, (14) on the map, and watched the moon rise. First it seemed like a star shining thru the trees. Then the rim came over, & the trees were silhouetted against the moon. It had the appearance of a rounded haycock. As it sidled up over the mountain the man-in-the-moon was the plainest I have ever seen it. We were soon asleep.

June 24

We had our coffee and oranges and then a
cold breakfast of corn flakes and milk that
we got from an Indian across the bridge,
Mrs. Bone. With George Barney, a boy
from the "neighbors," we made a hike
up the road toward Peter's Creek, down
a road, up the hill, across the ridge away,
down into the valley of Peter's Creek,
and home. Up a valley, (15), we went to a
spring and I had a pleasant time squeak-
ing and seeing Canada warbler, mourning
warbler, red-eyed vireo. As we had come
along road we had seen two rose-breasted
grosbeaks singing blithely from tree tops.
There was hot walking on the tracks,
and we left them as soon as we came
close to the hill. In a sort of valley we ate
beans and bread & butter, (16), and then
did some tough bushwhacking straight
south up the hill. At one "resting" place
a blue-headed vireo came and looked us
over, staying within a yard of us. We came
out at the top, (17), and had a good view
but wandered about quite a bit looking for
the trail marked on the map. [marginal
note: I climbed a tree & saw into Wolf
Run Valley.] We flushed a ruffed grouse
& her flock, and she put on a show for
us. I saw a blue jay. Finally we wandered
on using map & compass and watching
hill contours when we could see them.
Once in a while the "trail" was fair & we
did succeed in keeping it, such as it was,

pretty well. As we were climbing along the top of the ridge we flushed a pair of grouse with their young. One old bird flew first, almost straight ahead of us. Then suddenly we saw the other, along the trail, about 12 feet to our right, and we saw her plainly as she stumbled with her broken leg and helpless right wing. The young had flown off. They looked like a bevy of bobwhite. Once the old bird seemed to turn on us and charged as a hen does toward one threatening her chicks. She made a distressing cry for a while and then circled back toward where she was, clucking. At about (18) we clambered over a great many great rocks, some of them grown over with moss, blueberries and even brush. We were on the lookout for rattlesnakes, and George was hoping to see one to shoot with his 22. I had a hard time all day keeping him from shooting —first at a killdeer that started across the road in front of us and later at the grouse and other birds. So up at the rocks George shot at some kind of large garter or green snake and hit it right in the neck. We started down the hill toward the setting sun and were delighted to come on a little spring. We had been dry for a long time. There we rested and a blue jay came & watched us. We soon struck Peter's Creek, or a branch of it, and followed deer trails & the creek on down until we came to the remnants of an old woods road. Once we heard a deer's bark & we saw many fresh tracks but no deer. At about 19 we stopped and I built a little fire & Alice prepared dinner. We cooked cocoa on a stick supported on prongs and roasted wieners. Then as dusk came on we headed homewards toward the sunset, getting to George's house a little after 9. We visited a bit with Mrs. Barney & got into bed just as the moon was again rising over the Round Top, but this time quite a ways farther east. We were soon asleep, very tired.

June 25

I awoke with a sore muscle in my back. I think I caught cold night before by forgetting to put on sweater soon enough after taking off pack to make fire along Peter's Creek. Alice did most of work in packing bedclothes and doing up mattresses, etc. We had our coffee & oranges, later corn flakes, & just before we left we ate some bread & butter & jelly. George helped us pack. Jerome Bone came to pick strawberries and gave Alice some. I think he came too to see our camp, because he looked it all over with a gleam in his eye & seemed to admire it.

We pushed off about 10 o'clock with Bone watching from the bridge. George was up on top of the bridge, his mother & sister watching too. The river was fine, a current, interesting riffles, and clearing up so we could see a bit too. The sun was

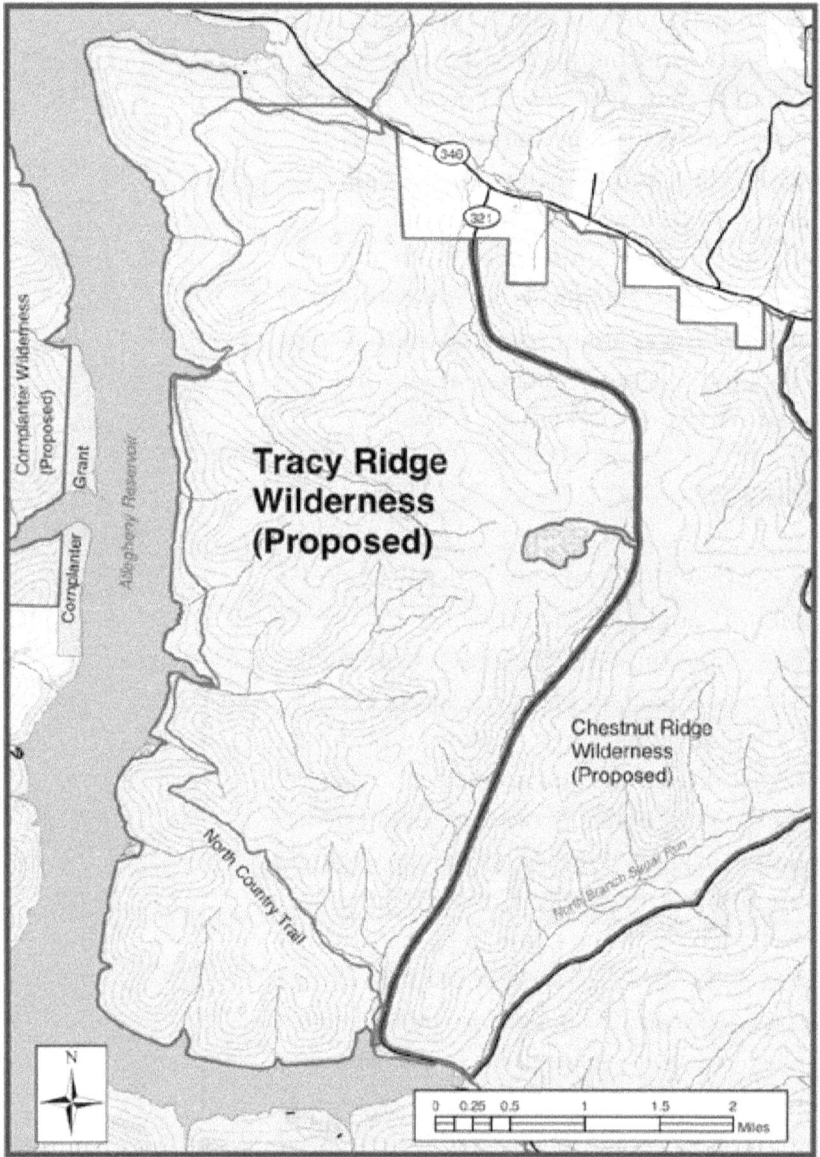

The proposed Tracy Ridge Wilderness Area, composed of the largest inventoried roadless area in the Allegheny National Forest at more than 9,700 acres. The Pennsylvania Chapter of the Sierra Club identified this tract as a prospective wilderness area in 1973, and Friends of Allegheny Wilderness took up the baton by incorporating it into their Citizens' Wilderness Proposal for Pennsylvania's Allegheny National Forest in 2003. Howard and Alice Zahniser canoed past this area on June 25, 1937.

bright. All afternoon & evening we frequently saw great blue herons flying high
above to far-off hills, skimming over the
river, standing in riffles while we passed,
or taking off just ahead of us. We passed
Corydon soon and were looking for Cornplanter Falls that Bone had told about,
when we came to Tracy Run, where we
had eaten on Memorial Day with Helen
& Aunt Jessie. We pulled into a cove just
above the stream's mouth. A boy was
fishing there. We went on down & landed
at the mouth of the stream, (20 on Nat'l
Forest map). A trailer camp there. We
visited. A young fellow told me deer were
plentiful at the lick up the run, said 25
had been seen there at once. We ate by
the stream — ham sandwiches & peaches & run water. A phoebe's nest under
the bridge that had had young birds in it
Memorial Day had eggs in it. After a bit
we pushed on and passed the Cornplanter "Falls," riffles no worse than we had
passed before. Soon afterwards we saw
an Indian hoeing in a field on the right
bank & I called to him: "Is this Cornplat-
er Reservation?" He yelled: "Yea." We
followed the right bank, even going to the
narrow, riffle side of islands, looking for
the Cornplanter Memorial but missed,
either because it was hidden from view or
because the river required too much of
our attention. But at the lower end of the
reservation, about across from Gowango,
where the hill comes steeply down to the

Looking north up the Allegheny River valley just upriver of the former town of Kinzua, now inundated by the Allegheny Reservoir. Howard and Alice Zahniser canoed this *stretch of the Allegheny River on June 25, 1937. Photo is courtesy of the Bradford Landmark Society, and was taken by aerial photographer Don Tanner in 1957.*

river and there seemed to be no clearing or road, we saw a bald eagle ahead of us flying to our right from along the river up higher into the hills. It came facing us first and then we saw it from the side. It was a beautiful mature bird, and we saw plainly the white head and tail. (21 on map)

As we saw Kinzua's houses we landed in a quiet cove to get some films. When we walked out to the road we found that we were 1 1/2 mi. from the store. So we hiked it, got 3 rolls for $1, ate butterscotch sundaes, 30¢, and at grocery store got wieners, sardines, & mustard, 45¢. (22 on map?) As we were walking down we had a beautiful view of a great blue heron flying over us from the river to hills away to the east, and as we were going back we saw 3 bobolinks and a yellow warbler. It was about 6 o'clock but we pushed on, hoping to get to an area in the Warren quadrangle, for which we had Geological Survey maps. We had expected a storm, but all had quieted down & the sun was behind the hills on our right. We came to Big Bend and took the riffles on the inside & came around to see the sun setting down the river valley of high hills. It was 7.30, and we landed behind two cottages where large rocks are along the bank, 23 on Geological Survey Warren quadrangle. The sunset was beautiful, golden on the river a stream of gold & I took a chance on a photo. I built a fire, & Alice cooked salmon and peas & made tea & then roasted marshmallows. I pitched the tent along the rocky waterfall from a mountain stream & blew up the mattress while Alice did dishes. Pitching the tent & blowing up mattresses took me just 8 minutes, done about 10.30. Then I made the beds. The moon came up through a notch in the hill up the old ferry road & we retired at 11 & were soon asleep to the music of the waterfall.

June 26

We got up about 8 & about 9 had a cup of coffee with the lady in the cottage. I had walked back around the bend—a big one all right—watching the outside, where the river is deep and quieter than on the inside of the islands where we went. I built a fire and Alice cooked bacon & eggs, & we ate about 10. Alice did dishes and made up beds while I studied maps & wrote this far in journal since leaving Onoville. It is a hot bright day, but this a.m. we are in shade. We watched a train go by—a fast freight with a passenger car on the rear. Yesterday in Kinzua we saw a "cute" little geared locomotive still in use but a relic of old lumber days—now used by a chemical plant up Kinzua Creek. We are beginning to think about ending our trip at Tionesta or Oil City. We pushed off about 12 with a hot sun, and enjoyed the scenery in this part of the valley, probably the best yet, the hills forming in general a steeper valley & the channels about the islands being swifter but not frightening. Quite a few cottages. Again we saw great blue herons and I saw a large hawk or an eagle marked under the wings somewhat as a turkey buzzard is. As we came near Glade we stopped on the right bank. As we were landing a bull-frog, big fellow, jumped into Alice's end of the canoe and for a moment we were in danger. The frog soon settled down in a sheltered place and I got him out later. A catbird was singing on a nearby treetop as eloquently as a mockingbird. When I squeaked he promptly came directly down to look us over. I shaved, and after a brief rest we pushed on, about 2. [Marginal note: Took photo here, too.] We came to Warren in an hour or so and had the ex-perience of the change industry makes in a beautiful river valley. But across from the business section the riverbank is a beauti-fully sodded and treed park. We stopped there and I spent about 2 hours getting some cash and buying sheets and towel, $2.27 and apples and cantaloupes, 54¢. We ate a bit and pushed on. The bends in the river were interesting and as we went to the left of Meade Island we came on a large dredge & an immense dredged area. There were rapids approaching it and then strange swirl and eddies as the current hit the deep water. The left of the island would have been more interesting

as the river there follows a wild, wood-
ed, steep mountain side with pine trees
and many slides. The sun all through this
section was laying a broad, blinding beam
on the water that made all the riffles more
surprising and exciting. We kept to the
left of all the islands through the Warren
quadrangle. After passing Grass Flat Island
we came into the Youngsville quad. A boy
was fishing at the mouth of the Broken-
straw. We had seen a workman walking
along the high bank on the westward bank
as we were leaving the suburbs of Warren,
an amazingly imposing figure against the
sky—especially his feet as he lifted them
in a steady walk and each was silhouetted
against the sunset sky. The river after Grass
Flat Island became even more beautiful,
and we enjoyed very much paddling along
southward with the sun just below the hills.
We landed at the upper end of Thompson
Island (26 on map) on a gravel beach. With
driftwood I soon had a tolerable fire and
we made coffee, cooked corn, and roasted
wieners. [Marginal note: Had cantaloupe
too.] We had no bread. I had little trouble
in putting up the tent on the gravel, and
we were in bed before 11 and had a lovely
time after a hard day. We could hear small
footsteps about us—cottontail rabbits &
mice. A car parked across the river. The Allegheny Highway was not far away, and we
could hear cars passing frequently. But the
good sound was of the river on the gravel
bar, and of small fishes or crawfish piddling

about the shallow water. All day we had seen many fish jumping out of the water. As we landed on this gravel bar a green heron waited at the tip until we were very close, but I was too busy with the canoe to watch it. As we were eating a wood thrush sang its evening song.

June 27

I awoke at 5 and went out to see what the day was like. Saw a cottontail scamper away through a flood path in willows & soon another—a small one—came scampering down another path toward me. There was too much mist & I went back to bed & slept until rain awakened me at 8. It was just beginning & had I started things earlier we could have been on our way before the rain. We got right up & packed the bedclothes before they could get damp. I soon had a fire and coffee & Alice fixed cantaloupe. Then we had cakes & bacon. I got more driftwood and soon had our first large fire. We sat in the tent while it rained. All morning a catbird has been singing. I saw a small mouse—I think white-footed—scamper away from food as I was taking the poncho off to replace some foodstuff. A sandpiper flew across stream. Early in the morning when I looked out I saw a sandpiper on the tip of the point. We decided to [push] off after one shower, and I waded out to load the canoe. As we started the rain stopped.

I took two photos just before starting. It was a fine day for canoeing—overcast sky but warm, not hot. We passed many cottages. One fellow shouted out to us about a rock, but I doubt that he realized how little depth the Alisonoward requires. Another fellow advised the left channel about one island, & we took it and scraped a rock in some riffles—for the first time but with no damage. The hills were beautiful, and here & there were clumps of laurel still in full bloom. One clump was just across from our Thompson Island camp. We saw great blue herons. I followed one with the field glasses and watched it in the top of a tree. Another we saw catch a fish, & this one we followed down the river for quite a ways, as it kept moving on by stages. Finally it crossed the river ahead of us, and we got a good side view of its maneuvering with long legs and long neck doubled together as it landed. The next time we approached, it flew upstream and we saw it no more. The bottom, gravel & rocks, was close to us in many places today & there were many interesting riffles. In the deeper, quiet places fish frequently jumped out of the water. As we came along an island near Magee, we saw a storm coming up. Alice put on raincoat & I a poncho. It turned out to be a heavy downpour. As we came to the tip of the island we saw cottages on the bank and a landing place. A group in bathing suits were just putting out. I had

Alice get to the cottage & started myself
to sit out the storm. But it was too heavy
and looked too much like a long rain.
So I ran up to the cottage, too. It rained
a steady, hard downpour for about an
hour and a half. As we sat on the porch I
looked at maps and read Emerson's essay
on "Nominalist & Realist." We found that
the people in the cottage had just dropped
in from Punxsutawney for the afternoon
& that the cottage belonged to folks in a
neighboring house. We decided to stay.
The name of the lady who owned the
place was Mrs. J. B. Engle, Route 1, Tidioute, Pa. (They rent cottage at $10 per
week.) Her son was very kind to us. We
paid $1 for cottage. While watching rain
from porch, I saw two large white birds
flying over the river. Seemed somewhat
like gulls and yet like hawks or pigeons.
Impressed me as something mysterious.
Later in the evening I saw a whip-poor-
will flying about over the river. There was
a beautiful evening. I read Thoreau till
dinnertime, after eating a can of sardines
as soon as I had carried the duffel from
canoe to cottage & spread out tent to dry
on porch. We had beans and wieners and
bread. Here, as in many places, we heard
bullfrogs plainly. We were soon in bed, but
a bed did not feel as good as our rubber
[air] mattresses.

Howard Zahniser retrieving an axe from the
Alisonoward during the June 1937 canoe trip
down the Allegheny River.
Photo by and courtesy of Alice Zahniser.

June 28

We were up about the regular season, and
I made a coal fire, and Alice made coffee
and griddle cakes, with bacon. I took card
up to mail it, & said good-bye to Engles.
The evening before when I was up for
water I talked a bit with young fellow
and a man who used to live nearby who
had walked through woods during storm
for a visit. He had his shoes off, had an
interesting face, hardly opened his mouth
when he talked. Alice took a picture as I
was loading canoe. After eating peaches,
bread & milk we pushed off about noon
and had a very pleasant & mostly easy
ride to Tidioute. There we stopped and
Alice went up and got about 75¢ worth
of groceries. We paddled on, finding the
islands interesting. It was a clear blue June
day. The sky was especially beautiful, with
cumulus, cirrus, and stratus clouds all day.
As we went under bridge at West Hickory,
after winding way through islands (once
we had to backtrack and cut through to
left channel), we saw two eagles flying
high over the "narrows." We stopped below the tannery to stretch. The canoeing
from Hickory on had the added interest
of the faint recollection of familiar things.
We were much interested in fish jumping
and in the green herons, one standing on
an anchored boat. A duck flew up from
the river as we neared Tubbs Run's mouth
and circled high in the air in ascending

spirals and up Tubbs Run Valley. We
watched the sky a great deal. As we came
near Tionesta we followed small currents
close to the left bank, despite shallow
water, as we hoped to land at the cemetery. But we missed it. We followed the
bank on down, passing the islands above
the bridge, took the channel back of "The
Island" and sought to camp there. It was,
however, too muddy there and chickens
were using the area under the one accessible tree. So we went on up Tionesta
Creek. There the water was clear and we
could see the bottom even in some depths.
It was a good paddle, and we camped
just above the bridge on land owned by
the Sundells. A yellow-throat [warbler]
welcomed us. I went up on the hill for
firewood, and we had hamburg, corn,
peas, bread, cocoa. [Marginal note: While
we were cooking meal George S. brought
us radishes.] I walked into town while
Alice made up beds. Cashed check for $3
at Hale's & bought eggs, bacon, oranges &
belt at Kilmer's for 42¢. Saw Ben Charles-
ton & 2 bros. there. Further down street
I learned that Harold had been through
with our car. Tried to phone him. Had a
good walk back to camp. The stars were
clear & numerous. I was pretty tired by
the time I got back. The fireflies made the
stream banks seem like a city. Alice was
abed, and I was soon there and asleep.

June 29

There was rain when I wakened at 6, but it was over by 7 when we got up. I built fire and got breakfast of coffee, oranges, shredded wheat, bacon, eggs, bread & butter, and Alice packed up things. Another storm was coming up but we were all packed & had things under ponchos before it arrived. The rain lasted only 10 or 15 minutes. We saw a mole along the road and I attempted 3 photos. We ate egg sandwiches and drank milk and pushed off. We had to paddle vs. wind, but it was clear and beautiful weather. We made it up the current back of "The Island" and landed among boats at the end of the bridge near Hoovers. We were not sure at the time that we would go on to Oil City, but this was the end of our canoe trip.

Howard Zahniser kept this journal of the canoe trip he and Alice Bernita Zahniser took on the Allegheny River in June of 1937. Unbeknownst to himself, their first child, Alison Howard Mathias Zahniser, was also along on the trip.

Journal Copyright 1980,
Atlantis Rising Communications
Post Office Box 955, Shepherdstown,
West Virginia 25443

Foreword and notes Copyright 2014,
Friends of Allegheny Wilderness
220 Center Street, Warren, Pennsylvania
16365

Notes on the Text

June 12: "Top is down" — The Zahnisers drove convertibles because Howard was a lifelong birder, even while driving. "Frederick" Maryland; "Greencastle," Pennsylvania.

June 14: Palgrave's Golden Treasury of English Songs and Lyrics (1861) is an anthology of English poetry that was selected by Francis Turner Palgrave.

June 15: Oil Springs Reservation of the Seneca Nation of Indians, Cattaraugus and Allegany counties near Cuba, NY. The Seneca used the oil for medicinal purposes. Allegheny/Allegany are variant place-name spellings.

June 16: "From filling station near bridge" over the Allegheny River at Olean, NY, where the canoe trip began. Zahniser called gasoline stations "filling stations." "This is marked 2 on our map." Unfortunately the map does not survive.

June 18: "Riverside Camp" presumably the Boy Scouts' abandoned cottage.

June 19: "field glasses" i.e. binoculars.

June 21: David Henry Thoreau, A Week on the Concord and Merrimac Rivers. This was the book Thoreau went to

Walden Pond to write as a memorial to his brother John. John made the canoe trip with Thoreau but later died of lockjaw from a razor nick. Thoreau's birth name was David Henry, which he later reversed to Henry David. Ralph Waldo Emerson was born Waldo Ralph. Margaret Sarah Fuller, editor of the Transcendentalist The Dial Magazine, was born Sarah Margaret Fuller. It is a mystery why no doctoral dissertation has sought to explain this phenomenon.

June 23: Quaker Run entered the Allegheny River from the east 1.25 miles south of Quaker Bridge. The reservoir created by Kinzua Dam inundated this area, including much of the Cornplanter Tract, land reserved to the Seneca Nation of Indians by treaty.

June 25: ". . . when we came to Tracy Run, where we had eaten on Memorial Day with Helen & Aunt Jessie": Helen Zahniser, Howard's younger sister. Friends of Allegheny Wilderness has developed in this area — on land now above the Kinzua Dam reservoir pool level — a proposal for a 9,705-acre Tracy Ridge Wilderness Area. Extending 6.5 miles along the east bank of the reservoir, this is one of the largest undisturbed areas in the Allegheny National Forest. All of the land surrounding the reservoir is sacred to the Seneca Nation. Much of the area is heavily forested in oak, white pine, hemlock, and other species. This is high-quality habitat for Allegheny Plateau wildlife, including bald eagles, who nest throughout the area.

June 26: Allegheny Highway — PA Route 62. Today, within sight of the Allegheny Islands Wilderness Area just upriver from Tionesta, a Pennsylvania State historical marker describes Howard Zahniser's work for wilderness preservation. Just down-river from the historical marker, Zahniser is buried in Tionesta's Riverside Cemetery.

June 27: ". . .scraped a rock in some riffles—for the first time but with no damage." Alisonoward was an extremely lightweight, wood frame canoe covered in canvas and therefore susceptible to damage.

June 28: Harold Zahniser was Howard's younger brother.

Note on the editing: Silent edits have been made to regularize some punctuation, to correct obvious misspellings, and to spell out possibly confusing or obscure abbreviations.

Appendix A

Below follows the testimony of Howard Zahniser from a hearing held by the Pittsburgh Office of the U.S. Army Corps of Engineers at the Warren County Courthouse in Warren, Pennsylvania on May 15, 1946 regarding proposals at that time to construct dams along and canalize portions of the Allegheny River.

On the Allegheny River

I have been told that all who come to Warren and go on up the Allegheny River to study the area around Kinzua go away with the impression: "It's too bad to have to do anything with such a beautiful valley." And that, I understand, includes engineers and many others whose reason for visiting the area is to see what CAN be done to this valley. I too say it is too bad to have to do anything with it, but if something must be done I wish to suggest some important values to have in mind when choosing between the alternatives.

I speak as the executive secretary of The Wilderness Society, a nationwide, non-profit, nonpolitical organization with headquarters in Washington, D.C., and also as one who has known and enjoyed this valley since boyhood. We of The Wilderness Society believe — with the support of an increasing number of

Americans throughout the country — that the more natural an area is the greater is its stability and long-time value to its inhabitants. Our prime concern as a society, our distinctive interest, is in preserving the remnants of the American wilderness free from all artificial developments, but we believe also that on all natural areas the artificial measures should be held to a minimum. In this fine, still highly natural valley of the upper Allegheny we would say, adopt only an absolutely necessary program of change and then hold the artificial measures in such a program to a minimum. Personally I would recommend that the proposed detailed navigation survey be made and that it include careful attention to the recreational values of this area.

There are not many valleys like this upper Allegheny left in the United States. For those who know it, it has great sentimental value. Some men are at times likely to call sentimental values impractical and to substitute for them what they call "practical" considerations. Yet men fight to preserve their sentimental values, fight and die for them, and to the nation their service in doing so is a highly practical thing. There is something practical too about recreation. The strains of our high-pitched civilization are such that the provisions for recreation in natural areas are becoming more and more a matter of social concern. As individuals we know already the tonic values of getting away from it all and recuperating from nervous tension in quiet natural scenes. It will not be long before we will all recognize such excursions as matters of real practical social concern, and we are going to need our quiet valleys more and more. Yet right now we are doing the impractical thing of making such areas fewer and fewer.

From Warren to Salamanca the Allegheny valley can well become, with proper planning and restraint in development, the scene of a kind of recreation that would be unique in this region. There is now pending in Washington a proposal for a bill that would establish "wilderness belts" or belts of wildlands along interstate stretches of mountain ranges and river valleys. If this bill is successfully introduced in Congress and enacted, this Pennsylvania-New York stretch of the Allegheny might well become such a belt of wildland for hikers from as far away as Pittsburgh, Buffalo, Baltimore, Washington, Philadelphia, and New York who would wish to traverse the trail between the railroad stations at Salamanca and Warren. There is no such provision for the increasing number of hikers in the entire East. The nearest thing to it is the trail system along the tops of the mountain ranges, and I am sure that an Allegheny River trail would far surpass any mountain trail in enjoyment for many hikers.

The value of this stretch of the Allegheny River for canoeists has never yet been fully realized either. Canoeists go far away to the canoe country of Minnesota. They go into the Adirondacks. For many of their purposes they could find nothing better than the upper Allegheny — as I once found out to my great delight when my wife and I, finding it impossible to travel to Canada or Minnesota, spent three weeks with canoe and pup-tent on the upper Allegheny, from Olean to Tionesta. Dr. William N. Fenton of the Smithsonian's Bureau of American Ethnology has described in the Living Wilderness a one-day canoe trip that he with his wife and Charles E. and Richard B. Congdon of Salamanca made from Salamanca to the State line in 1941. In his article, called "A Day on the Allegheny Ox-Bow," copies of which I have here, Dr. Fenton says, "Surely anyone who could have made even this one-day voyage with us might have been aroused to an appreciation of the still existing natural features of this valley, not forgetting the present Indian inhabitants. Conservationists will have many things to consider, when they come face to face with concrete plans to inundate this quiet, wild valley of the upper Allegheny."

Such considerations, I trust, will be very much in mind when the decisions are finally made with regard to this valley. However we may be compelled to deal with flood waters, whatever provisions we may find profitable for navigation to improve our transportation system, we certainly should do everything possible to preserve the heritage of natural beauty we have here for recreation, enjoyment, and inspiration. Such scenes are getting fewer and fewer, and our needs for them are becoming greater and greater.

Appendix B

November 6, 1963

The President
The White House
Washington, D.C.

Dear Mr. President:

I have been interested in the Kinzua area
of the Allegheny River for some time, not
only because of the scenic values that led
The Wilderness Society long ago to pub-
lish a descriptive article but also because
of a perhaps somewhat personal interest
in the Seneca Indians.

With this explanation may I not urge
upon you the most careful consideration
of the situation in which the Seneca Indians now find themselves? This concerns
not only their financial and economic well
being but also many of the values that we
usually speak of as spiritual. In all respects
it seems to me that we the people of the
United States owe them the most sympa-
thetic consideration.

The particular matter that leads me to
write you at this moment concerns the
relocation of the cemetery and the monument that are at present on the long-re-
spected Cornplanter Reservation that is
destined to be confiscated and flooded by
the Allegheny Reservoir.

I have just read in full a mimeograph duplication of the correspondence between representatives and associates of the Indians on the one hand and the Corps of Engineers on the other hand, attached to a news release of October 27, 1963, from President Merrill W. Bowen of the Cornplanters' Corporation with headquarters in Salamanca, New York.

The substance of this seems to be that the Corps of Engineers insists that the Indian cemetery become a part of another, a non-Indian cemetery on the far side of the imminent reservoir, while the Indians wish to have the cemetery moved to a site on their present side of the reservoir. This site, they believe, will be more readily accessible to them by road, will be theirs alone, and will include grounds for some of their traditional ceremonial meetings.

It has been personally embarrassing to me as an American citizen to read this correspondence and to sense the kind of treatment that a branch of our Federal Government is giving these Indians.

I want to add my personal endorsement to those appeals that I know must already have reached you with regard to this matter, and I may add that I trust that an improved attitude in this respect will also characterize the further dealings with these Indians with regard to their property

and financial rights. We the people of the
United States should be as generous with
them as we well can be.

Sincerely yours,

Howard Zahniser
Executive Director and Editor

HZ/lt

cc: Mr. Wilhelm Zimmerman, Jr. (2)
        Mr. Arthur Lazarus (2)
        Congressman John Saylor (1)
        Victor Taylor (1)

Appendix C

Pittsburgh Post-Gazette
Sunday, September 5, 2004

Tionesta native had hand in 1964 Preservation Act

By Ben Moyer

Forty years ago last Friday, President Lyndon B. Johnson placed his signature on the National Wilderness Preservation System Act of 1964. But it was the pen of a Western Pennsylvanian, Howard Zahniser, that fashioned the heart and soul of the law that would lead to eventual designation of 107 million acres of wilderness on federal lands across the country.

Zahniser, a native of Tionesta, Forest County, wrote the original draft of the Wilderness Act in 1956 as director of the Wilderness Society. For eight years he guided the law through 66 revisions toward passage by Congress. Zahniser died in May of 1964, days after testifying at the final congressional hearing on the Wilderness bill and four months before Johnson's signature made it law. He was 58.

"He'd just go and go, often 30 hours at a stretch," said Zahniser's wife Alice after his death. "In the end he just spent himself out." On Aug. 27–29, 13 canoeists in eight canoes commemorated the Wilderness enactment anniversary with a three-day canoe trip on the Allegheny River. Friends of Allegheny

Wilderness (FAW), a non-profit group based in Warren, organized the journey as part of its work to promote appreciation of the 9,031 acres of designated wilderness on Pennsylvania's Allegheny National Forest.

After a study of other relatively undisturbed parts of the Forest, the group proposes that an additional 54,000 acres merit wilderness designation. FAW faces opposition, however, from commercial forestry and oil and gas industry representatives who maintain that extractive industries are foundations of local economies in places such as rural northwestern Pennsylvania and it is unwise to bar such activities from federal lands.

According to FAW executive director Kirk Johnson, the group's proposal for additional wilderness on the Allegheny is not an attempt to stop timber or gas and oil production there.

"Our proposal is not an all or nothing proposition," Johnson said. "We have objectively identified the most wild, undeveloped areas of the Forest with the fewest conflicts for their potential inclusion in America's National Wilderness Preservation System."

FAW's commemorative canoe trip launched at Warren (canoes and shuttle supplied by Allegheny Outfitters, www.alleghenyoutfitters.com) and paddled 40 miles downriver to Zahniser's hometown of Tionesta where his grave, marked by an uncut stone from the forest, overlooks the Allegheny. Making the trip with Johnson were Zahniser's son Matt Zahniser of Covington, Ky.; grandson Dave and wife Rachel of Covington, Ky.; Stuart Zahniser of Erie; Julie, Dan and Gabrielle Kennedy of Clearfield: Charlotte and Will Ford of McConnellsburg, Nathan Bell of Bradford; and U. S. Forest Service wilderness ranger Eric Flood.

Under the rim of the Allegheny Plateau, the paddlers glided through the Allegheny River Islands Wilderness, one of the more unique areas in the nationwide system of designated wilderness lands. The Allegheny River Islands Wilderness contains seven islands totaling 368 acres embraced by the river between Warren and Tionesta. Named for early settlers, the islands are covered with forest and dense understory vegetation. There is no development and the islands are used primarily by fisherman and for camping by canoe parties. The FAW party camped in hard rain on Crull's Island and King Island along their route. Courson Island, also part of the Wilderness chain, can be seen from the Tidioute Overlook along the Tidioute-Warren Road just east of Route 62.

Friends of Allegheny Wilderness chose a canoe float to commemorate Zahniser's contributions to the wilderness protection because he and Alice had made a similar but longer canoe trip on the Allegheny from Olean, N.Y., to Tionesta in June of 1937. Howard kept a journal during the trip and recorded sightings of wildlife and vegetation. Their route took them along a section of the Allegheny that was later inundated by the Kinzua Dam reservoir after the dam was completed in 1966.

Zahniser's early life along the Allegheny and his 1937 canoe trip with Alice strongly influenced his conservation work in the next 27 years.

"We paddled on, finding the islands interesting," Zahniser wrote in the journal. "It was a clear blue June day. The sky was especially beautiful, with cumulus, cirrus and stratus clouds all day. As we went under the bridge at West Hickory after winding through the islands, we saw two eagles flying high over the narrows. We stopped below the tannery to stretch. The canoeing from Hickory on had the added interest of the faint recollection of familiar things. We were much interested in fish jumping and in the green herons standing on an anchored boat."

As Alice and Howard Zahniser did in 1937, the FAW flotilla encountered numerous bald eagles, blue herons and abundant waterfowl. Ranger Flood asked the group to "help the Forest Service" by keeping a lookout for a possible eagle nest among tall white pines near one of the wilderness islands. A mature eagle soared out of the forest near where the nest was thought to be, and an immature eagle stretched its wings on a snag downriver, but the canoeists did not spot a nest.

Two miles above Tionesta, Johnson led the fleet ashore below the rumble of log trucks and the rush of tourist traffic along Route 62. There along the west shoulder stands a blue and gold Pennsylvania Historical and Museum Commission marker dedicated to Howard Zahniser's work on behalf of wilderness.

"It is quite fitting that he be mentioned in a place where not only did he have some of his most formative years, but in a region where there are two wilderness areas designated already," Matt Zahniser said.

The Hickory Creek Wilderness is the Allegheny National Forest's other designated wilderness. It consists of 8,663 acres of northern hardwood forest atop the plateau above the river's east bank. Both the Hickory Creek and the Allegheny River Islands areas were granted wilderness designation through the Pennsylvania Wilderness Act of 1984.

Together, their acreage amounts to less than 2 percent of the Allegheny National Forest total, far below the 18 percent of national forest land designated as wilderness nationally. Most designated wilderness is in the West, but according to Johnson protected wilderness on the Allegheny is scarce even compared to other eastern states.

"Demand for wilderness experience in the Allegheny National Forest is very high and the available supply in the region is low," Johnson said. "The Allegheny is Zahniser's home national forest and the inspiration for Friends of Allegheny Wilderness' efforts stems from the fact that there is so little wilderness in his home forest. We believe we must do his legacy proud by protecting what would still amount to a small fraction of this forest. We have an obligation here to live up to the hard work that Zahniser put into wilderness and its protection for the entire nation."

Reprinted courtesy of the
Pittsburgh Post-Gazette.

HOWARD ZAHNISER (1906-1964)

Conservationist and architect of the National Wilderness Preservation System Act of 1964. Although he died four months before President Lyndon Johnson signed the bill, his efforts led to the preservation of over 100 million acres across the nation. Zahniser was born in Franklin, Pa., and Tionesta became his hometown. An advocate for preserving wilderness areas, he was executive director of The Wilderness Society and editor of its journal.

Howard Zahniser's son Mathias, right, and grandson David, left, at the Pennsylvania Historical and Museum Commission marker for Howard Zahniser two miles north of Tionesta along the Allegheny River during the August 2004 40th anniversary of the Wilderness Act canoe trip with Friends of Allegheny Wilderness. Baker Island and No Name Island, of the Allegheny Islands Wilderness, are close by. Photo by Ben Moyer.

www.ingramcontent.com/pod-product-compliance
Lightning Source LLC
LaVergne TN
LVHW091208080426
835509LV00006B/897